I'm Just Saying

Unfiltered

A Poetic Prescription

Composed By

Milton McCulloch

The Bethune Group, Inc.

D/B/A
Bethune Publishing
P. O. Box 2008
Daytona Beach, FL 32115
Phone: 386-265-3733
docbethune@tbginc.org

Because of the dynamic nature of the Internet, any Web Addresses or links contained in this book may have changed since publication and may no longer be valid. The views expressed in this work are solely those of the author and do not necessarily reflect the views of the publisher, and the publisher hereby disclaims any responsibility for them.

Library of Congress Number: 2016900985

ISBN: 978-0-9971548-2-5

Author photograph and cover design by

John-Mark McLeod of
J2maginations, LLC
j2maginations@gmail.com

Printed in the United States of America

I'm Just Saying

Unfiltered

A Poetic Prescription

Milton McCulloch

The Bethune Group, Inc.
d/b/a
Bethune Publishing House
732 Orange Ave
Daytona Beach, FL 32114
386-265-3733
docbethune@tbginc.org

Copyright 2015 Milton McCulloch

All rights reserved. No part of this book may be used or reproduced, taping or by any means, graphic, electronic, or mechanical, including photocopy, recording, taping or by any information storage retrieval system without the written permission of the publisher except in the case of brief quotations embodied in critical articles and reviews.

Table of Contents

	Page Number
Dedication	8
Forward	9
1......I Plead the Blood	11
2......Eyes Have not seen	13
3......My Legacy	16
4......The Freedom We Seek	18
5......Call It A Day	20
6......In Demand	21
7......Forty-ninth Year	23
8......Chocolate Eclipse	24
9......Dat Body	26
8......Wow-man	27
9......Expectations	29
10.....Reflecting On Some Things	31
11.....Within The Midst	33
12.....Weighed My Options	36
13.....Eye Contact	38
14.....Dis Journey	39
15.....Dreamer On Top Of a Hill	42
16.....Power Of the Sheath	44
17.....Each Day	47
18.....Count to Three	48

Table of Contents (cont.)

	Page Number
19.....Breathe	50
20.....Suicide Spirit Shall Not Prevail	52
21.....Scandal	54
22.....Calling Me a Bitch	56
23.....Miss P in Red	58
24.....Pain	59
25.....R.I.P. Dad	62
26.....In Retrospect	63
27.....Escape to My Love	64
28.....I am Woman, I will Roar!	65
29.....Amber Alert	69
30....Commonality of Death	71
31....Beautiful Woman	73
32....You Told Him What	74
33....Perm Without A Permit	77
34....Speaking My Mind	78
35....A Voice To Hear Us	83
36....Falls	87
37....Inner Demons	88
38....Solid As A Rock...I Am Solid	93

Dedication

Thank you my friend, thank you my brothers, thank you my sisters, thank you my many mentors, thank you my many role models...

Thank you Chris for being there for me with a meal many days when I had it so tough, you are a true friend...

Thank you Homer for being a spiritual brother who has always loved me unconditional, never judging me...Your prayers are felt.

Thank you Rodney, a son to love forever...

Thank you Putus, a mother I love and who loves me so much...

Thank you Glen, I still feel your presence in my life...

Thank you PSlim, your forgiveness and friendship is truly appreciated...

Thank you Lord Jesus...There is none like You!

Forward

Greetings:

The poetry and prose of Mr. Milton McCulloch is refreshing, thought provoking and insightful. As a woman, I read his words and wonder how he can know so well the inner thoughts of women. But as I reflect on his upbringing, I realize that he has existed in the female energy field since birth. He has allowed himself to become a stronger man by not being afraid to feel and express that connection.

Pieces such as, Eyes Have Not Seen, Suicide Spirit Shall Not Prevail, Calling me a Bitch, are anthems of empowerment. They resonate with women across cultures and around the world. We all know that when a person is really trying to stir up your anger or make you feel bad about who you are, the first word out of their mouth is to call you the "B" word. Milton, speaks to snuffing out the heat of that flame simply by looking at the source and giving it no power.

Cloaking sexuality in the Power of the Sheath, brought a smile to my face as I remembered, in agreement. I laughed out loud when I read Breathe. It reminded me of what my mother used to tell me when I was stressing about something, that time would fix. Milton has managed to see the inward thoughts of women and put pen to paper with words to express many of those unspoken words and wishes. He expresses, with great passion, the determination, yet the sometimes, lonesome yearning of the soul, for victory, love, gratification, companionship... or just a touch.

Life experiences, headlines and words spoken in confidence are reflected in the written word of "I'm Just Saying! Unfiltered" You will connect and reflect but most of all you will want more.

So, sit back with a nice glass of your favorite wine or milk and cookies if you prefer and enjoy this journey filled with expressions of feelings that you or someone you know has familiarity. Take it in, let it marinate and then savor the taste as you fully engage the senses and allow yourself to feel the energy of the writer as he paints the picture with words.

Loving the Arts, in the Spirit of Dr. Mary McLeod Bethune

Dr. Evelyn Bethune "Sweet Pea"

I Plead the Blood

Dem think seh mi ignorant of dem plans,

God see dem an everytime dem mek a move

Fi destroy His intentions fi mi life,

Him just restore mi wid His hands....

Di Lord is my Shepherd

Many, many ways I walk,

At times a stray from di path

He set out fi me

And then come the haters wid dem talk,

"Cawe she naah live right

God haffi a deal wid har",

But mek dem keep casting dem stones,

I'm not a bastard child

Fimmi God and me still a par!

Di Lord is my shepengaleng

In the midst of my troubles

He's ever so near,

When ole devil spit at me him poisonous venom

I will neva fear,

When him offer mi pretty fruit

Saying, tek a bite

It naah go do yu no harm

Chu, listen to me nuh mi youth...

Say, get away from mi Lucifer

Yu ole ancient trickster,

Yu don't mean mi any good,

Be thou remove,

I plead the Blood, the Blood.

Eyes Have Not Seen

The heavens have opened up to reveal a secret,

Listen, observe and understand,

The skies are not randomly being dressed

In blue, white, grey or rainbow colors,

The truth has always been within our reach,

We have just retreated from it….

The rain journeys from the ground

Unnoticed to our busy schedules

And on its return journey to wet the earth

Find some asleep,

Asleep while the cumulonimbus clouds

Gathered their mass, and

Nestled above our existence, as we

Squabble over frivolous things

That will neither provide meaningful substance, or

Lead our essence to such hope that brings

True relevance to our daily purpose….

We wander aimlessly like an arrow

Shot from a bow by unskilled hands,

Cowards who acknowledge, but

Will not face the adversaries of our souls,

Oh! Eyes have not seen!

Walk down the streets of your neighborhoods

And you will see

Betrayal is cloaked in loyalty,

Love has abandoned a home,

And trust is filled with tears,

A child speaks to selfish ears, saying,

"I don't understand why"….

To what is, and what has been,

Only God can make it clear to our spirits,

Ears have not heard, and

Eyes have not seen.

Through your walk in this life strive to walk good with others. However, your walk in life will be accompanied by others whose intention at times is to either support your dreams or thwart your progress.
IJS...Bryan Mac

My Legacy

My legacy will be my voice,

My voice will speak from my heart,

My heart will seek to have a voice

That will not choose to be silenced

When I need to be heard,

Even if most refuse to hear

And a few are inclined to listen,

I will be His oracle to generations present

And generations to come,

My voice will be remembered

For the words I wrote,

The kindness I spoke,

The love and devotion I showed,

I don't want my flaws to be forgotten,

But to be forgiven,

I want my voice to continue

To resonate beyond my grave,

To encourage those I have left behind

And instill a sense of hope,

Invoke actions that will make

Others realize that in this life

One should live in the present

In a manner to affect tomorrow

And not continue to live in the yesterday…

So, my legacy will be my voice,

My voice will speak from my heart,

My heart will seek to have a voice

That will speak beyond the words

"I love you"….

The Freedom We Seek

The freedom we seek is sometimes the bondage we gain,

The freedom we seek doesn't always

Brings strength to those who faint,

Sometimes it will weaken the oppressors of our will

And give resolve to those who are oppressed,

The freedom we seek

Sheds light on the reality

Of what lies beneath the ills,

The freedom we seek is more than just words,

It's a sense of truth that will last,

It's in the present that we live,

Not in the future or the past,

Freedom is not legislation written to appease

And right the wrongs of the nights,

To ensure the present and the future is devoid

Of any attempts to deny my basic human rights,

Freedom doesn't give you the privilege

Due to your preconceptions of my hoody,

To mistake me for an agent of malevolent nature,

Confront me with a thought

And intentions to be the master of my freedom,

Some will never get your motives

When you took my life with the power of a weapon!

The freedom that we seek has now made us both victims,

I am really free Zimmerman,

You are forgiven,

You took the life from my body,

But couldn't touch my soul,

And caused the hearts of those who love me

To be angry and be cold,

See what your actions brought,

For one, your freedom to also walk as you please,

A major increase in hoody sales,

I am laughing out loud!

And some significant attorney fees….

Yet, from this view that I now stand today,

I stand with the revelation of what true freedom means,

Free of anyone's suspicions

Because of the color of my skin,

Free of each day and week

Of the racial tones with which some speak,

Free of the expectations

Society sets for me to live,

Free to look at you,

I dare you to look at me!

Free to never be in bondage again,

My blood is on your hand,

I no longer seek to be free

I am singing freedom songs,

Free to know who I was meant to be,

More than a boy named Trayvon….

Call It A Day!

Five days have gone without a call or text,

Now you're standing at my door

Asking me what's next,

I would let you in but I'm busy,

My time is at this moment occupied with a guest,

Bout to watch a Redbox DVD,

Three's a crowd,

I got 911 on speed dial

So don't be like in the past

Get upset, boisterous and loud,

In case you're wondering

If you've been replaced by another,

I can save you the worries,

But on second thoughts

Just stand there for a while and ponder….

Now, go spend more time with your boys

You're always hanging out with, or

Let me guess

Tomorrow you'll be working an extra shift,

I am so over you,

You're like a tire that is so worn

And clearly has seen its last mile,

That must be replaced,

I am so not stressing over you,

You're like an old building

That has been condemned

And must be demolished to make room for

A new building to take its space…. Call it a day!

In Demand

Mi get up dis mawning bout 5 o'clock,

An before mi cudda even open mi eyes good,

Mi two children dem a call,

An mi husband a beg,

Tek one before yu gone,

Di day barely start an mi in demand!

A woman's wuk is neva dun,

Even if yu wuk a regular fulltime job,

It seems like enuff hours nuh in di day,

Dat's why each day mi haffi pray,

Before mi tun di superwoman switch on,

To mek it thru another day I'm in demand.

Barely have any time fi pamper miself,

Always a put everyone first,

Mi boss a wuk call after hours,

A want fi tell her at times wey fi turn,

Come Friday, chardonnay brings mi some calm,

And relief di stress of being sooo in demand.

Weekend come wid its expectations,

Church folks start fi badda mi soul,

Dem a try get mi inna dem passa passa,

Dat's Jamaican talk fi gossip an drama,

Laawd Jesus! Tek mi case in Yu hand,

Keep mi tongue, dat's all of You I demand.

So, I've been seriously thinking of late,

Tu mek some demands on my terms,

One weekend a month mi a gu pon vacation

An do nothing roun di house,

Have hubby, children at my command,

Mek dem know how it feel to be, in demand!

Laaawd! Ha, ha, ha, haaaa!

Forty-ninth Year

My soul rages in the night,

Struggles with the dark,

Walking thru a tunnel

Where there seems no end in sight,

Pieces of my heart are in pieces,

I say, 'Let them be',

My hurt will be viewed

That I make it all about me....

Fell asleep by five,

Awoke by nine,

The cameras are still rolling

In the forty-ninth year of my life,

My heart is all shattered,

I am so done,

Felt like enough years on this earth

Lord I want to go home....

I hear the voices

Of opinion

From center, left and right,

You experts,

Here's my opinion,

Please leave me be for a while...

Voices from all angles,

Like they really know all the right answers,

Maybe you should apply it to yourselves

And heed your own advice.

Chocolate Eclipse

There is more to me than what your eyes see,

Beyond the white teeth that my beautiful smile exposes,

Beneath the delicate balance of my soul

Between expressions of intimacy

And a heart that constantly reveals

Its depth,

Its power,

Its desires

In any language,

There is more to me than what your eyes see,

I am not just a piece of sexy chocolate

You fancy solely for your feminine pleasure,

Sugar mama,

Cougar,

Young pretty thing,

Stamina like a stallion,

I'm your sex slave

All night long

Hard as a rock,

Six foot three,

Breed from Shaka Zulu stock,

There is more to me than what your eyes see...

Your desires rise to my nostril,

You hunger for my hip movements,

Which I fulfill without any chasm,

To what end?

Even when a greater part of me says, no,

I always concede….

Cease to disparage my thoughts,

There's more to me than what your eyes see,

Close your eyes

For a moment be blind,

Abstinence infused,

Let your imagination run wild

With the inoculated visions of

Chocolate that is being savored

For just that right moment,

I am more than what your eyes see,

Sincerely yours….

Dat Body

Dat body you got have me standing to attention,

Got my heart beating, got my blood racing....

Dat body you possess is quite a fine sculpture,

Display it in my museum for my private viewing,

Dat body you acquired needs the warm gentle touch of my handling,

Bring dat body come girl let me show you how I'm working!

Wow-man!

Is this how we should feel

When we have found the person

For the rest of our lives,

Especially when you thought

Those before were the permanent thing,

In between the experiences

Of the temporary,

Not going anywhere,

Not marrying your flings,

Is this how we should think

When your heart feels like

This is so finally right,

And no matter how you try to imagine

Life without her,

It becomes truthfully clear

There can be no other,

She is your missing rib

You have finally awoke to find

In her nakedness,

Exuding beauty you've never seen,

There is none fairer in your eyes,

None more beautiful than

Your queen,

Inspiring such awe,

She is the epitome of a wow-man!

This is how you should feel,

You want to break out in an exuberant dance,

Do the bogle, the chicken scratch,

Moonwalk around her,

Boogie soul train style,

Shouting Woooow-man!

Like a wild man-child,

A dance of joy,

Celebrating this true love

That you have found,

Sing a new song,

Smile at the sound of her voice,

Give her your whole heart

To care for,

Watch her fold it like freshly washed clean white linen...

This is how you should feel

When she walks next to you,

Adorning your daily space,

Filling it with what you need

When two become one,

Making you the envy of every man,

God in the midst,

She is as I said the epitome of a WOW-MAN

Expectations

Expect me,

Expect you,

Expect us,

Expect to,

Write n chat

On a social website is a fun thing to do,

Expectations,

When you kiss your boo,

You know what

I'm saying,

Like socks

In a shoe,

Like a rainbow in the skies,

And truth that expose lies,

Expectations

Is part of the

Dynamics,

In the process

Of life...

Give today a chance to give to you. Give thanks with a grateful heart. Give yourself more credit than others will give you. God gave everyone a gift to share with the world, so don't ever think it's any less special than other's more celebrated gifts. You are unique and God created no one else exactly like you. Love some you today like you've never before. God loves you.

IJS.... Milton Bryan Mac

Reflecting On Some Things

I am not black

I am not proud

I am not colored

I am not too loud

I am not da man

I am not your boy

I would care less what you think,

How you feel,

Your opinion matters not to me,

I am not your nigga,

We're not blood

We not family!

Missed read,

Misrepresented,

You're not an option I care to explore,

One, two, three

And counting,

Booty call is next door,

I am not your woman,

I'm certainly not your hoe!

Look into the mirror

You'll see who's for sure,

Where did you come from?

Who let you out?

Liar, Liar!

You're a dog,

Go chew a bone!

So I sit here reflecting on some things

That lately hit me in the face…..

Within The Midst

When I look up from within the midst of my surroundings

I sometimes wonder why You love me Lord,

Why after I had oft let You down,

Failed so badly in giving You pleasure,

Acting like I can do it on my own, and

Yet, denying that I do so,

Why won't You forsake me?

Even when at times I hide behind a cloak of spirituality,

Afraid that I might not be accepted for my flaws,

And my vulnerability will be exposed,

Ripe to be taken advantage of

By that which fights against Your divine will for me,

My own flesh! That part of my tripartite being,

I remind myself of John 3:16....

Why do I still struggle with finding myself,

And seek to conceal any pain I feel inside,

Oh, You're my Jehovah Jireh, Rapha,

And much, much more.......

From the rising of the sun and beyond the evening dawn,

When I look up from within the midst of my surroundings,

I sometimes wonder why You love me Lord.

When You look down from your glory

Nothing misses You from Your vantage point,

Charging Your angels with orders, dispatching

Them like super agents to do a super job

Of supernatural proportions on behalf of a people

Who were not a people, but are now a people,

I am a witness of Your power...

Your power to save, to heal, to forgive,

To see beyond all my excuses

And the skeletons in my closet,

I cannot take back the things I have said and done,

I however can regret, repent of past actions,

thoughts and words spoken,

Repentance is such a key component

To bridging the levels of our relationship,

So, when You look down from Your glory,

Why do You love me Lord?

This walk with You should be so easy

If I have faith as small as a mustard seed

I will be able to move mountains,

Rise up out of my valleys,

Cross the deepest seas,

Conquer all my fears with the power that now lives in me

And resurrected the Son of God from the dead...

Speak to me Lord in the midst of my surroundings,

Speak to my neighbor who cloak

Their struggles with an "alleluia"

Dance and shout down the Sunday morning "Soul Train",

Ever cognizant of the observers they try to sway

With this outward show that "I'm" right with God,

The truth is never far away.....

As we look up to You from the midst of our surroundings,

Cause our hearts to cry "Abba Father!" again

With the innocence of a child who knows,

Really knows,

Knows....

His Father.

Weighed My Options

I have weighed my options,

It's a no-brainer,

Get ready!

It's gone on much too long,

At forty years old

I'm graduating from

You weighing me down,

Struggling with your fluctuations,

Enticing my palate with

No respect to boundaries,

Stretching my externals,

Refusal to adhere to rules,

The more that you gave me

The more that I would lose...

I am ending this shindig

This whole shebang

Has been a fraud since day one...

"Call di doctor fi mi",

Doctor Spencer prepare

The knockout concoction,

I got a patient for you,

Some things must go,

I've got high expectations for my life

And I will not accept no,

"Call di doctor fi mi"!

A woman's got to do

What a woman's got to do,

I have made a decision.

Some things have to finally go.

So you in the mirror,

Yes you!

I called the doctor today,

Soon and very soon

I will be telling you goodbye,

That's a fact,

Won't miss you,

And I don't want you back!

Eye Contact

I saw inside your soul beyond the colors of your pupil,

Like peering through the window of a seaside cottage,

Never failing to capture the events unfolding as the sea waves

Washes the face of the beach shore,

Pondering the calculated dynamics of nature,

I saw you just as evening were coming to a close,

As I wandered through life's daily corridors,

Meandering, avoiding, and negotiating

All that I was meant to face,

I never saw you coming,

I never saw you looming….

We have met somewhere before, right?

I can't recall exactly where,

It seems like my memory can't shed any light

Of your previous travel to destinations where I had existed,

Where eye contact would have embedded your body shape

And prevented this dilated search to find the truth…

Dis Journey

From di day yu wuz conceived,

Til yu popped outta her gut

And mek yu first sound

When di nurse smacked yu likle butt,

And in some a oonu case

From day one til now,

Mama has always been dere

Though daddy wuzzin roun.

 Thru breast milk, Infamil, porridge,

Bacon, fried eggs, toast,

Rice and peas,

Bammy and fish,

Mashed potatoes,

Brown stewed chicken,

Curry goat, rundown,

Yu sucking every piece a meat

Off dem oxtail bones.

 Thru soothers, runny nose,

Belly aches, nightmares,

Potty training, first day of school,

Don't figet when yu was teething,

Thru all those baby years

Of yu four main things,

Eating, sleeping, pooping and peeing,

Mama wuz a constant

She neva stop believing.

Memba wen stampede

Happin a National Stadium

In di seventies and yu bawl

Cause she neva mek yu go,

And di neighbour cross di road

Likle bwoy lose him life

In dat crazy rush,

Looking back I realize,

A shudda neva mek such a fuss

It wuz not dat Mama

Neva wanted mi fi have some fun.

Memba getting in trouble

Cawe yu stayed out too late

And neglect fi du yu chores

It wuz not a pretty fate,

An at sixteen years of age,

Think yu wuz too grown,

Den Mama drop lick a yu skin,

She said, "Yu think yu too ole"

Wipe dat frown off yu face,

Just wait until yu have a few

Kids of yu own.

Dis journey has not been easy

Thru di trials and di tears,

Thru di fears and di failures

Thru di good and bad years

If yu mama still alive

An yu can touch her wid you hands,

Lift yu voice an tu di Father

Give Him praise and plenty thanks!!!!

Yet fi some, mama has sadly

From dis earth been gone,

Yet dis journey still continues

Cause her memory lives on….

Dis journey continues

Cause her voice lives on…

Dis journey continues

Cause her spirit lives on.

Dreamer On Top Of a Hill

Imagine swimming in a pool of milk

Living a life of luxury

Submerged in sands of gold

Travelling to famous cities afar,

Rubbing shoulders with the "in-crowd",

Awakened to mornings served breakfast

On a golden platter,

No concerns with a tight monetary budget,

Oh, how I dream of the many ways

Such a time will arrive

Before your last breathe,

Last grip of the present fades

To remain with me

Far beyond

The decades….

Imagine living most of your fantasies,

Looking back with no regrets,

Fulfilling many lifelong dreams,

Loving life to the fullest,

Imagine

Bucket list almost complete,

Dreamer, or

Realist…..

How many can say

I've live my life trying to succeed

Instead of

Trying not to fail,

Dreamer on top of a hill

Laying on top of a 1600 thread count

Egyptian sheet,

Where there's a way

There's a will

I am carried by persistent feet,

Ascending to the top of the hill….

Power of the Sheath

Since the Genesis, men have
Yielded to the seductive power of the sheath,
Having succumbed to the subtly sophistication
Of the sweet sounds and smell emanated,
Inherently disguised to gain
The trust of the most secure of humans,
Luring them into a cave of historic
Irrelevance, falling away
Into the past of obscurity
Never to regain their former glory,
Another mighty warrior fell…., who's
Influence has been diminished
To less than a mere whisper of yesterday,
Recipients of pleasures for a moment
Without much thought to what
The consequences would bring….
Certainly, one would expect brilliant minds
To ably discern the effects of the affection of
The power of the sheath,
Learn from those whom have
Preceded throughout the ages
Filled with arrogant delusions
And in the end became conquered victims,
Not the first
Won't be the last,
The future is ahead,
Be prudent now,
For what's to come
Will one day be the past,
The sheath is stealth,
Black, white, or a silhouette of complexions

Covered with a patch of receptacles, or
Reflecting a desert surface,
Enticing, delightful to the view,
Strong, resilient, soft to the touch,
Raw, defying the conventional definition of
Outward beauty,
Exacting very little effort
Yet gaining so much,
Causes masculinity to swivel
Into a posture of weakness,
The sheath has power
That many men have sought
And failed to keep,
Of which mighty armies of ancient times
Were brought to their knees…
In modern times examples exist,
Ask an ex-champion, who has battled,
Won a world title in the ring,
Then boasted there's no man
Bad as him alive on planet Earth
He cannot beat,
Only to discover it's not a man
But someone in the form of a woman
Possessing a sheath.

*D*on't get hung-up on others pointing out your flaws/imperfections just because they may not be your favorite person, true haters of you or folks who you don't think highly of. It's difficult for most of us to acknowledge such messages from these messengers and like Balaam they seem like an ass trying to impede your life. Listen to the ass braying and you may begin to understand that God sometimes needs to use even the most unlikely person or means to get you to see the truth. (Numbers 22). So just shut up and listen (Proverbs 17:28)....

*E*xamine your humility today and you may be quite surprise how much you really need to grow in this area of your life. Be more honest with you today in certain areas of your life...Anger, kindness, gentleness, alcoholic problem, unhealthy eating habits, selfishness, don't work well with others, doesn't listen well (hear but doesn't really listen), think you're better than others (think because someone lives in a tough/rough hood they don't have high ambitions, very smart and are drug free), treats others mean...etc. Have a blessed "Being honest with myself" day.
IJS.....Milton Bryan Mac

Each Day

Each day you are alive

Is a chance to continue healing,

Each moment there's breath in you

It's for you to see the path

Laid out before the beginnings

Waiting for your hand to grasp,

Each day you feel broken

Is an opportunity

To experience getting through

Another day, so

You can be grateful

For reaching this far,

And reach towards the possible

That's always been in your sight,

Let your eyes see the unseen

Beyond the celestial star,

Each time you speak

It's a window to initiate life not death,

Each time you hear the pessimistic wind,

Listen to the sound of your own breathe,

Then feel your soul,

Live, love, learn and do your best,

For any worry about tomorrow,

The morrow... Will take care of the rest....

Count to Three

'Putus' once told me,

"*I brought you into this world*

And I can take you out of it",

This same person would also say,

"*I'm going to count to three*",

I needed more time then,

So she could have counted to ten,

Typical old school Jamaican parenting,

You understood

That was a promise

And every word she meant,

Eat your vegetables,

Eat it all

Before any rice and meat,

Saturday mornings had its occasional

Unwanted treat

Of that forever voice

Belting this dreaded command out,

"*Yu color doesn't look too good*",

So you're taking a washout!

That was basically a torture of your taste buds!

Consuming that "washout" tea is

One reason why Jamaicans are so quick,

As we had to sprint several times

In a day to make a number two deposit!

I guess I've spilled

The secret to the world,

It's not just the food we eat,

Not us outrunning gun bullets

That has made Jamaicans fast as "Bolt"

And an Olympic sprint "Beast",

Genetics may play a part,

All part of a Creator's grand plan,

The truth be told,

For a tiny Caribbean island,

To land some first place gold.

Breathe!

Summer may find you lost beneath the shambles of choices

Awaiting the Fall to again descend with an awakening

Of great expectations adding to past years

That have accumulated nothing but

An overwhelming feeling that has reached

A summit of unimaginable proportions,

I hear voices

Crying out for recesses from a troubled life,

Praying….breathe,

Take a moment to breathe!

You gave and gave and gave

Unconditionally from the first moment,

Someone took a piece of you

They may have thought

You would never regain…

But you will resurface above the dismantled,

Chaotic opinions of naysayers

Your ambitions will eventually surpass theirs,

Watch my words!

So my friend….breathe,

Take a moment to breathe!

Release him finally from your bosom,

You are his wife,

Not his husband,

Not his mother!

He can't handle all your great womanhood,

The show has ended eons ago,

It's going to be all good,

So my sistah….breathe,

Let her run wild to

Who she thought would be a better catch,

When she tries to return this time,

She will find you with your soul match!

So my brotha….breathe,

Take a moment and breathe!

Tell that friend to breathe,

She has held onto that baggage long enough,

Release it and breathe,

Mama it has been so rough,

Just breathe,

The bills may still be here tomorrow,

So just try to take a moment if you may to breathe,

Don't hesitate now,

And breathe,

Release,

Breathe….

Suicide Spirit Shall Not Prevail

I will be the canvas that inherits

The skillful strokes of an artist who

Delved deep inside his soul

To unearth a masterpiece that will last

Forever in the thoughts of history,

I will be the stone

Whose potential was disguised

To the undiscerning eye

Until the hands of a sculptor

Chiseled away the waste, for

My beauty to be seen,

I will be the bridge that reaches

Beyond isms that have penetrated

Human behavior and made many prisoners

By another person's crave for power,

Blinding their hearts to the reality

Of how true love makes you free,

I will embrace the path beckoned for me to travel,

I will follow, I will lead,

I will dare to be the true me.

The suicide spirit that permeated my thoughts

Is recognized for who it is!

I lay siege to the thought that "I am a victim"!

I envision my end to be triumph,

I won't be a statistics of defeat,

The suicide spirit will not take my life

Nor forever shackle my hands and feet,

My circumstances will not be the determining factors

Of my outcome and income, nor will

The failures of a society,

I am owed nothing except

What I owe to myself!

The suicide spirit shall not prevail!

I am somebody

Who has ceased to say I can't,

I won't,

But will say as I continue

Along my life's journey

I can,

I WILL!

Scandal

Someone come to my defense,

This situation calls for a remedy,

Shaking my head!

The latest news,

I stand wrongfully accused,

Clearly a case of mistaken identity,

Making me out to be a perpetrator,

I am innocent until proven guilty!

Arms cuffed behind my back,

Led away like an animal to be slaughtered,

I'm mad! Embarrassed!

Hear my side of the story,

There's no truth to words rolled from their lips,

I got a witness who can testify

That I was not there

When whoever committed this crime,

She can clear my name,

It's their words against mine,

Nowhere near before your hell broke loose,

One ought to exercise better judgment

With the friends you chose,

If you think I would be so stupid

As to jeopardize my life in the free world,

I didn't do it!

Think about it for a second,

Although it has been only a few weeks

Since you've been an ex-factor,

Wasn't I good to you, this reeks!

Here's the truth,

Got a new girl,

And was home laid in my bed watching Scandal,

Enjoying a moment of fantasy

Swear, I swear it's not a lie,

Was making love to my girl on tv

But she wasn't making love to me,

Olivia Pope is my alibi!

Calling me a Bitch

Calling me a bitch,

You just don't know any better,

Calling me a bitch,

You wouldn't say that to your mother,

Calling me a bitch,

Won't change who you are,

Calling me a bitch,

Won't stop me from reaching for the stars,

Calling me a bitch,

Shows your inadequacy,

Calling me a bitch,

Cause' I took your trifling, sorry, pathetic behind

To court for child support money,

Calling me a bitch,

When I caught you between her legs

And your pants down,

Calling me a bitch,

Then why did you ran so fast

And for days went underground,

Calling me a bitch,

Answer your phone!

Calling me a bitch,

I am going to put an end to your derogatory tone,

Calling me a bitch,

So you finally come out

And still calling me a bitch

With a text instead of words from your mouth,

Calling me a bitch,

Hold up, unknown number calling

I wonder who it is

Calling me a bitch,

Oh hell no!

It's your aah….I will hold my tongue

That you cheated on me with!

You're both inconsequential,

She can keep your one way ticket sorry excuse for a man,

Note attached,

Don't return to sender,

So keep calling me a bitch,

You no longer matter,

And unlike you,

I respect my mother,

So I won't call you, a bitch!

Miss P in Red

It's me!
Nurse Paulette in my red blouse,
I was feeling fine
When I left my house
Dressed in a black skirt
With a subtle scent of
My expensive perfume,
Stepped out of my front door,
My neighbor's twenty year old son Andy
Couldn't take his eyes off me,
I was going to my nurse's Christmas Ball,
He gave me quite a chuckle
When he shouted across the street,
"Hey Miss Paulette,
You looking really good",
And if I needed an escort tonight,
Just say the word and he would,
Jump at the chance
To be with me,
Cause all those girls around his age
Can't touch me when
It comes to looking so sexy!

Pain

Pain….

Inflicted on my soul,

Penetrates the walls I created to protect me

I am a voice that calls that wails,

Only the eyes of God can truly see.

Pain….

I've kept close to my bosom,

Choosing to hold within,

Hidden from those I fear will not understand,

And, continues to control my emotional strings.

Pain….

I will not always have,

I sense from this hurt I'll soon be free,

Past, present, future is at stake,

I will surely sing again a voice assures me.

Pain….

Refuses to give into my desire

To be restored to a place of release,

And fly on eagles wings

With abandon freedom in the skies.

Pain….

The battle is not for the swift,

I close my eyes and listen,

My deliverance is at hand,

My soul has envisioned the end.

Pain….

I pray, I pray, I pray, I pray,
I hope and sense a joy,
I know my God will sing for me,
I know he will give me the victory.

Each of us have a fear. It could be a fear of heights, fear of spiders, fear of dating, fear of trying new things or a fear of failing....It's time to face your fears whatever yours is. You have not been given a spirit of fear, but a spirit of love, power and a sound mind.

IJS....Milton Bryan Mac

R.I.P. Dad

I sense your presence
In a way like never before,
Your flaws seemed
To have clouded my perception
Of what you truly desired to be,
A man who was destined
For such greatness
That you never fulfilled,
Your ashes speak
A message so clearly,
Your absence illuminates
My dreams,
Dad, I wished our partnership
While you were here was more than it was,
I wished what I see now,
I had then seen,
I wish you were here
Still fighting through your pride,
Holding closely to the
Hurts you desperately tried to hide,
No more Father's Day, birthday treats,
When we took timeout
Spent time together to eat,
You're in my thoughts dad,
Rest in peace....

In Retrospect

I will, I won't, I can, I can't, I delete, I cut, I complete,

I adjust, I see, I touch, I hear too much, I speak, I write, I wrote…

I'm good, I'm bad, I'm happy, I'm sad, I pray, I wait,

I inhale, I exhale, I aimed, I clicked, I hit, I missed,

I'm covered, I'm hidden, I'm naked, I'm seen…

I'm a lover, not a fighter, I'll love, and I will fight!

I laugh, I dance, I cry, I sing,

I'm mistaken, I'm corrected, fooled, berated,

About insignificant matters,

I'm hated,

I fall, I rise,

I fall and I rise!

Escape To My Love

I want to escape to my love,

Flee to where I cannot escape from,

And realize romance that won't cease to last,

Live in the love of your kisses, essentially...

Smile at the whisper of your voice,

Reach for the warmth of your embrace,

Like the horizon of a new day

That welcomes another sunrise

Greeted with fresh dew

Waiting in bated expectation

For the gentle kisses of the sun,

Giving credence to the truth

Our day will come...

I desire to escape to my love

And be captured to where I desire to not escape from,

Wake up to find that all is not lost,

That in the embers of life's flames, burning

Remains in the ashes survived remnants

Of an Argentina tango

Full of passion,

Daring to stay alive as it

Fights what seems like a losing battle,

The final moments beckon,

Then like a Phoenix

We ascend once more,

Rising with our love far beyond and above....

I am Woman, I will Roar!

Strictly Manny,

Not into Jenny,

Stance unshakeable,

Take it or leave it,

You got to be a pleaser

To fulfill my fantasy,

Knew what I needed

And how I wanted it,

To get me through

A night of unforgettable ecstasy...

Just turned five Oh,

Divorced with no kids living at home,

Ex-husband left me for a much younger version,

Living all alone,

Empty bed since,

My body yearns for a man's touch,

Been on the path of abstinence

Counting three years,

It's getting too much,

Seeking a man with the skills

That needs to change,

Toys are heading to storage

Time for the real thing,

Seeking a strong body,

Counting down to the final hour,

Hope he can handle the work

And bring the power!
Three months of consistent pursuing
Not even close to giving in,
Early morning calls of his sexy voice
Causing me to think things
A grown woman shouldn't be shy about,
Sweet Jesus, please keep me near the cross!
My pillows have requested that my thighs
Retire from the pleasures of squeezing
On a frequent schedule and leaving
Them to question the dual roles
Imposed due to the lack of romance in my life,
A pillow will not dictate to me,
I pay the bills for this living space,
When pillows get worn-out
They can be replaced,
Oh Lord
Keep me near the cross!
He tried to make me feel like I did him wrong, but
I am finally breaking through the fragile
Emotional crap that lingered with me
For so many years,
Struggling with my self-esteem
Not loving the extra pounds that first started
To assert themselves after three childbirths
And a need to satisfy my physical hunger
That was emotionally rooted,

I tried and tried in many ways

To concealed the deep hurt,

It was there for sure, but

I am woman

I will ROAR!

Back this story up,

Thought he was the bomb in bed

Maybe for the first year and a half,

So for a long time I let him believe this instead

Since he wouldn't hear my plea

That I needed him

I _____ NEEDED him to HEAR!

Lord I only thought it

Ok, I know I shouldn't swear!

But that man gave to the church

Faithfully his tithe, talent and time

And lived a lie at home

He never gave me mine,

I felt like a forgotten affection

No different than a piece of furniture,

His Mercedes in one day

Got more caresses,

More than I got in five years,

Twenty years of the same,

Me on my back

As his stick got hard and aimed,

Mission accomplished before the end of

A five minutes commercial break

Leaving me in a quiet wonder

As I waited for his snores to drown out

The buzzing sounds of the sure thing

And the shriek it emanated from within,

Words can't describe!

At times I believe

He pretended not to hear,

But I got to a point where

I no longer cared,

I just kept being the good wife,

Cooked and hosted Thanksgiving dinners,

Smiled with everyone

Like we were living the perfect life,

Always giving an Oscar worthy performance

While my unhappiness kept increasing,

We knew the truth,

The yearly façade

Was coming to an end,

Never would make it to two decades….

Roll back to the present,

I am not wasting another minute

Any more time

Trying to please a man

Who doesn't reciprocates,

I want much, I need more

I am woman,

I will ROAR!

Amber Alert!

Amber alert!
I kept driving pass the flashing message
Displayed above the highway,
Took some notice of the info
Another little soul could be hurt again,
The story will be televised
Across the news media stage,
Another family's heart is being ripped apart
Another precious child is missing,
I can't begin to imagine the pain,
To be in a state of hope or giving in,
The state of uncertainty
Experienced by any parent
Facing the possibilities of never seeing
That innocence, the smile of
Their child so effervescent…
This event should never happen,
Good concerned citizens organized
In waves of groups searching, hoping
To find a body still breathing,
Praying the near future will unfold
With tears of joy
For the little soul that was spared,
This should never happen,
Processing the pain of
A little soul that won't return…

Amber alert!

Days, even weeks may have passed

And every time the phone rings

Answering is such a heavy task,

Your presence is requested in the visage of a morgue,

It has been said,

No parent should ever have to bury their child,

But this is a reality

That everyone may have to live,

And if you never do,

Count it a blessing,

And if you did, this is me

Poetically speaking,

Sympathetic to your lost,

I believe there's still a God

I am just saying,

So if you feel like putting

All of your burdens on Him,

I know He can bear it

He's next to you listening.

Commonality of Death

Today he died the death of a president,

But won't be mourned by millions,

Won't have a national day of mourning

A commemoration seen by many,

She died just like everyone

And took a final breath,

Death will not mistake her identity

Death will know them by name,

Laughter will be heard throughout the land

In the midst of tears and aches

Will those we leave behind

Find the treasures of our life, and

Recognize the roots of our mistakes,

Commonality of men in birth and death

From lands near and far,

Born to live,

Born to die,

Let it be said….

Death at times seem like a logical, permanent escape

From one's troubles, but life provides a detour

Thru Hope Street....take it!

Beautiful Woman

For a moment I lend my ear,

The silence spoke

Louder to me than I intended to hear,

Beautiful woman,

Wonderful soul,

I know your worth,

You were first in heaven

Before you came to my earth,

God had you destined

Betrothed to the 'one',

Beautiful woman

So wonderful, so strong,

I will kiss your brow

Your eyes, your ears,

I adore everything about you,

Will love you for all the years.

You Told Him What!

You told him what!
I was going to call but
I chose to write you a letter,
Folks don't use this forum much, but
I believe it can be so much better,
Since you're such a smart person
I was careful to use proper grammar
So that I could be at my articulate best,
Microsoft Word tools in full use,
A finale statement to you from me,
Didn't want to leave room for any excuse,
Please listen and listen to me well,
I'm not the one!
I won't stoop so low,
Take your drama to E! News, or
Better yet Jenny Jones or The Jerry Springer show,
Where's Jenny these days?
Probably tired of people like you!
How could you tell him that his manhood
Is so small,
And expect it not to gnaw at his pride,
Your tact went throw the window!
It's going take a long, long time
Before he's playing show me yours
And I'll show you mine....
I've heard some crazy things before,

When this all went down
You weren't even having a lover's war,
And to add further damage to his psyche
You told him your last lover
Had an anaconda,
Now you have this man acting all crazy,
Harassing your mama's house phone,
Bordering on stalker tendencies
Tell a man this kind of truth
And it could be some serious drama!
So for the future
Thoroughly inspect the merchandise
And if you find they're wanting in a certain area,
Be sure you can live with your choice,
But if you can't,
Reflect on some history and just nicely walk away
For if you so insensitively mention me again,
Another of your relationships will have to pay.
Yet you still insist!
We no longer will have this conversation
And saying if he didn't want to know the answer
Then why ask the question,
You don't get it,
If you weren't physically fair to the eyes,
You wouldn't take kindly
Someone declaring that you sure is ugly!
We all know the truth can hurt,

You're not for real,
Wish you the best dear
Lay off calling my phone,
And I'll not be surprise to find
You in ten years, still all alone.

Perm without a Permit

Perm went lawless without a permit,

Hair, rogue style gone,

My crown just temporally lost it!

Don't call me Ms. Kojak

Cause like General McArthur

It will be back,

I am a Nubian queen

With great resilience

I just get stronger,

Count me out if you dare,

I am like a lioness

Protecting her cubs,

Courageous and fierce,

At 11 a. m. we'll start a fling

I'm going to sit in this barber chair,

Papi please do your thing,

I'll find a comfort zone

Clip away my friend,

I'm going to rock this do like Grace Jones!

Speaking my Mind

I should really speak my mind

On some emotions I feel,

Let some people know

In no uncertain manner

The repercussions of actions

Done to my race were very much real,

Their ignorance continues,

God help me understand,

Slavery of blacks in America was officially

Abolished in 1865,

Why can't they get this man!

Yet almost one hundred and fifty years later

There's a real denial among some

Regarding disparity between the white majority

And minorities in this country,

They say why black folks get so mad

They think we ought to be more thankful and satisfied

With what we already had!

Why you make most issues about race,

Affirmative action is not necessary these days,

You finally have a black man as President

See, Obama's proof enough racism in America

Has long come to an end,

Really, is that true!

Be a chameleon,

Change your skin color to black

And live for a while in my shoe

Here's a thought too,

I've never seen a Martin Luther King Jr. street

Running through a predominately white residential area,

A low income black neighborhood with a golf course,

But usually a token community center,

No troops were sent to South Africa

To free Nelson Mandela

No supplies of arms to the majority black South Africans,

No invasion to crush Apartheid, clearly then

A Weapon of Mass Destruction,

Established by a wicked regime

Descendants of your British cousins,

Sudan, Uganda, Rhodesia, Rwanda

Don't even count Grenada,

Bosnian War involved some of

The poorest white Europeans,

They got helped, why?

Anyone make a "white" guess,

Now think….

Haiti during and after the Doc years,

Don't let me go there,

Iraq and Iran war was about the oil,

A political scam,

Saddam was going down

Cause he wouldn't stick to the plan,

Again and again,

Seems like most times when

The democracy police

Have a hand in the welfare of Africans

It resulted in further enslaving them.

I'm speaking my mind,

Spoken word is my medium,

My destiny compels me to bring to light,

Woman suffrage movement

Highlighted more human plight

Women gained the rights to vote

Yet what are rights when things still ain't right,

Women continue to jab

With the good ole boys club,

Contend with hormonal jokes,

The reality is that the O.B.C.

Is threatened by the progressive female hub,

Beauty and brains can be

In the same packages,

Every woman didn't sleep their way to the top,

If not for women

Through the ages

We men would greatly flop!

Speaking my mind…

We are who we have become. Life changes us and we evolve into who we are by the choices we make along the way. We are who we think we are, what others think we are and what God knows we are. Seek to understand who God knows we are and make choices today that will make who we become will be a person, a people that will build and have great relationships, families, friendships and communities. WE ARE WHO WE HAVE BECOME.....
IJS....Milton Bryan Mac

A Voice to Hear Us

Long before King Rodney, Queen Rosa, King Martin and Queen Victoria

The struggle had begun,

On a fateful moment in Ferguson,

At other times too

A finger on a trigger ended

The life of another daughter or a son,

The cause, the motive, the truth, the reality speaks,

A parent's heart wails

Like a voice to hear us,

Yet its volume is muted

And what still exist are sleepless nights

Dreams that can no longer be realized

Hands held high,

Hands on the steering wheels,

Perpetrator apprehended....No, shot, killed!

Call it what it is,

From L.A. to Sanford,

New York to Georgia,

It's just plain murder!

Shot many times, a fatal bullet to the head,

Another soul cried repeatedly,

Another soul's voice they wouldn't heed

Another soul's voice ignored

Pleading, "I can't breathe, I can't breathe, I can't breathe, I can't breathe"!

Rules of engagement are rot,

Someone must be on top,

Law versus lawlessness,

This is not just about justice!

Unreliable eye witnesses seems to be the trend,

I suspect the message as much as the messenger,

Seek the truth to the end,

The dead can't recall or recant,

Refute, refuse, or speculate

Drive a car, ride a bike, walk the streets,

Chalk-lines transit to invisible state,

A people must walk the thin line between love and hate

While another mother's heart suffers crying out "Jesus"!

And silhouettes lose their voice to hear us,

The news conglomerates deceive,

Yet, they haven't broken our faith and will to believe….

Swing low, sweet chariot,

Coming afore to carry we home,

Marches, protest, rebellions,

Cause and effect and you expected

The people wouldn't riot,

You stripped the meat off our bones,

But we're too legit to quit,

Fought your wars and on our return home

Stopped us from whipping our ass in certain toilets,

"I ain't got no quarrel with no Vietcong"

But with a power of another color,

I've known my real enemy all along,

"No Vietcong ever called me a nigger"

"Burn this mothafucker down"

A father in such pain bellowed

And you're considering filing charges,

Yet, killed four little girls,

Burnt our churches down

Murdered us along dark roads

And never came back with a guilty verdict,

Numerous KKK hangings,

Ordered us to the back of the bus,

Rivers of your blood should have flowed all over this land

After you assassinated voices that heard us….

"Whites only" signs have been removed but still exists,

 "In God we trust",

Makes me a skeptic,

The subtle hypocrisy since integration,

Open your eyes, one must,

No more segregation, fill in the blank,

It is the same _____, different generation,

We need a voice to hear us….

Absent now are white sheets to barely conceal

The evil cowardice of their face,

Presently they hide behind political

And corporate America's place,

We have come a long way

Says the white guy in congress

Who grew up a conservative Republican,

Says the white guy in the Senate, a Democrat

That America belongs to Americans,

Forgot about the Native Americans

Whose land was stolen by visitors who entered without a visa?

Forgot about the Africans forced against their wills

On the cotton fields to do severe labor?

No National Holidays as a reminder,

Do what we must to always have

A voice to hear us….

Falls

Giving is getting,

Giving to you

I'm not regretting,

Getting you

Gets you believing

I'll be here for you

Freeing,

All that's stressing you,

I'm undoing,

As I'm touching you,

Kissing,

My lips exploring you,

Your body,

Kisses trailing every part of you,

Your glory,

Tasting,

So many sips of you,

Your Niagara....

Aaah, hmmmm,

There.....

I'm here....

Always here...

Falls....

Inner Demons

Inner demons unleashed a terror so unforgettable,

One needs a fresh reminder of better days,

There are memories some would gladly erase

And have those demons slayed,

Life happened without ample notice,

In one sudden stroll lives changed,

Souls cry seeking healing

Though repeatedly saying,

No! Should have sufficed

But never did…..

Girl you're a sexy thing,

So charming,

He made my heart sing,

Sweet words flowed so effortlessly from his lips

Lured me in like bees to honey

We were destined to be our only,

He was what I needed,

It seems like fate, but

As much as I wanted him

I determined we would have to wait,

Then out of nowhere hell's minions

Made their grand entrance dressed to kill,

Intent on destroying my will,

This was not a dress rehearsal,

The audience of one was for real,

He thought all those dinner and movie dates

The last three weeks were worth fair exchange

So like any game of Russian roulette

Inner demons were always calling his shots

And here surely to collect,

Ripping away my Garden of Eden leaves,

My Adam stole from his Eve

With rampant disregard to my virginity,

Inner demons invaded my body

Depositing dregs of their vile DNA,

Fear and shame held me captive for so long,

Too long for the proof to be evident, or

The crime to be relevant,

So as time passed my testimony was lacking,

Victim walks in bondage,

Attacker walks around freely living,

His words against mine,

It's down to he said, she said,

I recalled pinned to the bed,

Room felt like a prison wall

At no point was intercourse consensual,

I've had moments wishing I was dead,

My moon is dark, and the sun now rarely shines,

Inner demons seek to silence me

Like close encounters of the third kind,

Mirrors reflect my right as left, but

My image wouldn't want to walk in my shoes

I must find the strength to one day undo, or

Seek revenge like "The Accused"...

My story could have ended at this,

But God flipped the script, so

I'll never end up in certain statistics....

An awakening occurred

And suddenly all my shackles fell to the floor,

Inner demons grips were being dismantled

And losing the eternal battle for my soul,

The truth is, while God's eyes are on the Sparrows

He never forsook me even in my deepest of lows,

No matter how hard I tried to camouflage my inner pain,

Deep down I was praying to be saved,

Yet kept being the life of every party

Hiding behind any kind of wigs,

Being a real life Samantha Jones of Sex in the City,

Until those inner demons were cast into a herd of pigs,

Now inner peace reigns,

I am past the shame,

I don't point blame,

I am not the same,

I am not the same,

I am not the same,

I AM NOT THE SAME!!

Love I never knew like this before

Now resides in my heart

And all those inner demons have fled so far away,

I HAVE BEEN GIVEN A NEW START.....

       Look into the mirror of truth,

It reflects what you see

          And what you choose to ignore...

SOLID As A Rock... I AM SOLID

Solid, solid as a rock,
I'm solid, solid as a rock,
I've got mountains to climb,
Got rivers to cross,
I've got giants to slay,
Got valleys to walk,
Only so much more time
Before I spend my last dime,
Some battles I will lose
But I will win the war,
I've got dreams to live,
Got a whole life to give,
Truth reveals the lie
I was born to die,
Never again to live
On the other side,
You see there are two ways to live,
Two ways to die
Either for yourself or a Higher Power on high,
I'm solid,

Solid as a rock,
I am solid,

Solid as a rock,
You may think you live in a bubble,
Immune from any of this world's trouble
And guns, terrorism and power
Can't stop what's due some that hour,
Your disbelief can't change the truth
There's a Greater One than you,
Cause every knee shall bow,
Every tongue shall confess
What I'm saying is true,
So every time you take a life
Adding more sorrow and strife,
Every time you feel like
You can decide who lives or dies,

Everywhere your feet will trod
Is being seen by my God,
Can't you see the devil controls your mind,
How else could you kill
A defenseless innocent child!
I'm solid,
Solid has a rock,
I am solid,
Solid as a rock,
Start a new revolution,
Chose a different solution,
Sing a brand new song,
The tunes and lyrics have been so wrong,
Got to keep going on,
Get on the train to Zion,
It's a jungle out there
But I'm strong like a lion,
You see this hunger in my eyes,
It remains fixed on the prize,
I get derailed at times,
I get detoured at times
I get sidelined at times,
Lose my footing at times,
Yet no matter what I face
He has me still on His mind!
So I'm solid,
Solid as a rock,
I'm solid,
Solid as a rock,
What's behind the curtains?
The curtains of isms,
What lies behind the veil?
The veil of religions,
What's concealed in the dark and
Hidden from our sight,
One day will be exposed
By the truth of light,
While I am in this world,

It won't ever conquer me,
I'm from a lineage
A King's son,
I am ROYALTY,
This is no fallacy,
I have a great destiny,
I bleed red but
I'm from a great African legacy,
I'm solid,
Solid as a rock,
I am solid,
Solid as rock.
This road I travel got its perils,
And filled with all its devils,
The day will come when all the good in this world
Overcome all the evils,
Your neighbor could be your friend, or
Your true enemy,
In your despair a stranger could be there
Sooner than your family,
Read between the lines,
It's so black or white,
I am a realist,
It's never been about these rhymes,
My feet are planted on a rock,
There's no sand beneath,
I stand on a sure solid ground
I will never, ever sink,
My life is in His hands,
My trust is in His plans,
The devil is a liar,
God's word will eternally stand!
That's why I'm solid,
I am solid as a rock,
I am solid,
I am solid as a rock...
I am solid,
I am solid as a rock....

There is more to your existence…

                There is a divine plan for you…

Live to fulfill your purpose…

Live like there's a tomorrow,

Live like there's no tomorrow…

I'm Just Saying...

www.ingramcontent.com/pod-product-compliance
Lightning Source LLC
Chambersburg PA
CBHW070546300426
44113CB00011B/1803